SPRINGSTEEN ACCESS ALL AREAS

Lynn Goldsmith

UNIVERSE

Lynn Goldsmith

INTRODUCTION

This book is for all of those fans of Bruce Springsteen and the E Street Band who wanted to know what it was like to have full access during the Darkness on the Edge of Town Tour, what it was like to be part of a traveling ministry.

In 1978 there were those who thought Bruce was the savior of rock 'n' roll and those who didn't think much of him at all. Bruce who? But for fans, Bruce Springsteen was a holy rock 'n' roller, a preacher who could create a fervor in his devotees that would prompt them to spread the word about him as though he were the Messiah. His shows were more than a concert ticket, his albums more than party music. Bruce Springsteen and the E Street Band were a religion. People talked about Bruce as though he had saved their souls, as though he had given their lives purpose. The records and, more importantly, the shows seemed to trigger something very private—something that each person already knew about himself but may never have realized. It seemed to be about a shared sense of loss, an inability to fit a preconceived lifestyle, a restlessness. Fans told nonbelievers they must come to a concert—they too would be converted. All they had to do was get a ticket to one of the shows.

What was it for Bruce? For him life was about writing, making records, and touring. It was a do-or-die experience. Each time he went onstage it was an opportunity for him to connect. He needed it. This didn't mean that he was comfortable performing. In fact, he was afraid of it, but once he hit the stage, he was clear that this was where he should be and what he should be doing.

The beginning of the Darkness on the Edge of Town Tour was made up of small venues. The shows were sold out on both coasts, however in middle America few people had heard of him. In 1978 radio stations played music by artists such as Fleetwood Mac, Jackson Brown, and The Eagles. Because of Bruce's low singing register, he got very little mainstream radio air play. Halls that held three hundred people might only have sold thirty seats. The best part about seeing the show in those places was that Bruce and the band put out the same amount of energy for those few seats as they would for a full house of a few thousand. For the E Street Band, it was all about the experience they achieved onstage together. They were proud to be part of that music, to play with someone who worked so tirelessly because he believed in the spirit of rock 'n' roll. Because of the music the band knew that one day the crowds could be stadium sized, but they were committed even if that never happened. They were on the road to get closer to their believers, to have them spread the word, and to convert those who had not appreciated the music in previous shows. In this way, Bruce and the band transcended everyday life.

With each show, Bruce pushed the band to go further. After most performances, he'd meet with the band backstage and talk about what worked or what didn't. Bruce had many of the shows taped to see how they could be improved, and as the band traveled to the next town, Bruce would listen to the performance on the bus. Everyone would sleep a few hours until they'd roll into the next town at about 6 A.M. They'd check into a hotel, catch some sleep, then leave at about 1:30 P.M. for the hall. Bruce and the band would work out new ways of doing some of the songs for that evening's show. No two shows were ever alike. He always tried new approaches while keeping certain key moves and cues the same.

Bruce wanted everyone who saw and heard his show to be able to do just that. He acted as though it was his own family coming to the show for the first time. During the sound check, while the band played on the stage, Bruce would walk all over the venue, sitting in different seats, listening to the sound, and checking out what the ticket holder would be able to see. If he didn't think the seats were good enough, he refused to let the promoter sell those tickets. Seats behind the stage were never sold.

Sound checks went on for about three hours. Max's job seemed the toughest physically. Since the shows were always at least three hours long, it meant that he was drumming about six hours a day. He didn't tire. He wanted to be the best—not just for himself but for Bruce.

That was another of Bruce's talents; he could get other musicians to be their best for his music. They were part of something real, something they could respect, something that challenged them and gave them a positive image in the music industry, something meaningful. Bruce was not necessarily their closest friend; it was always clear that though they were all pals, he was still the "Boss."

It was a little different with Steve. If there was anyone in the band who could or would stand up to Bruce or just express his honest feelings, it was him. He knew he had a kind of brotherhood with Bruce that the others didn't. Still, he too would sometimes be careful around the "Boss."

On the bus, Bruce had his own space in the back. He'd watch America roll by the windows. Sounds glamorous, but it wasn't. Because the motor was in the rear of the bus there was a steady shake as well as disturbing engine noise. The other members of the band slept in tiny bunks in the middle of the bus.

Backstage, there were always two dressing rooms—a large one, with lots of food for Bruce and a much smaller one for the whole band. Few people ever came into Bruce's dressing room without being invited. This included band members. They could have, but they just didn't. They felt afraid of intruding on Bruce's thoughts. Rarely did Bruce go to their dressing room before the show. There were no group prayers, yells, or high-fives all around. His going to their dressing room was more about checking to see what they were wearing, especially Clarence. Bruce knew what he wanted them to sound and look like. You wouldn't wear anything that Bruce didn't want you to wear. Springsteen and the E Street Band were going to sound and look like a cohesive group of individuals.

About twenty minutes before the show, Bruce would get a time warning from his roadie. He'd often be listening to tapes of classic R&B artists that he carried with him in a small briefcase. He'd work out what he was going to say onstage and rehearse some moves in front of the mirror. He'd start to come alive. The band went on first, then a light would hit Bruce. It seemed he was brought out of the darkness to share his redemption from personal pain through rock 'n' roll.

As the tour progressed into the fall of '78, there were questions about performing in larger venues. Would Bruce play Madison Square Garden? This was a feather in the cap of any rock star, but Bruce didn't want it. He liked playing halls that at most held 2,500 people, where he could jump from the stage into the crowd. He wanted to stay in touch with his roots. Deciding to play The Garden was something he tortured himself over, but he finally decided to do it. Bruce had a long-time Jersey friend drive him to the show. He would never use limousines. He wanted to keep it simple.

Lynn Goldsmith

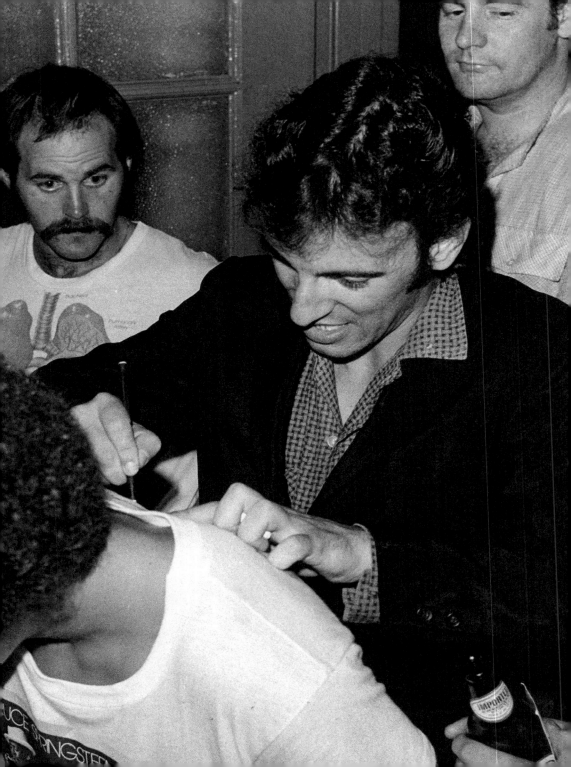

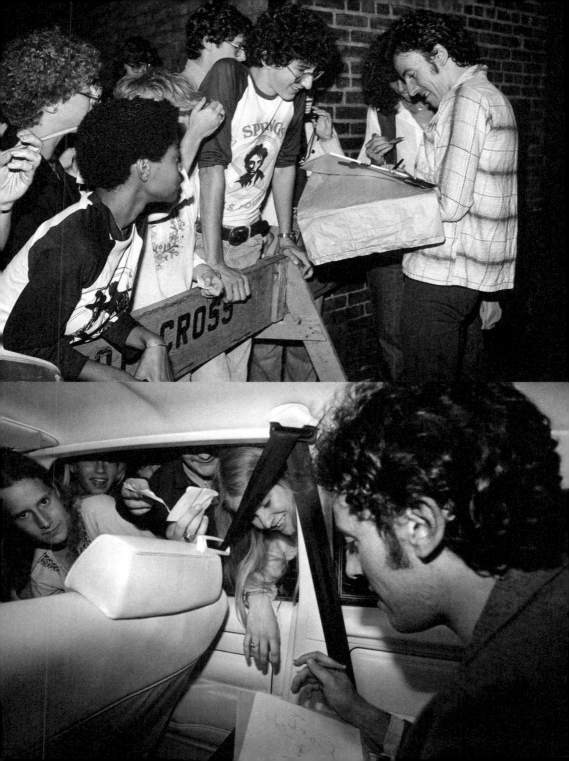

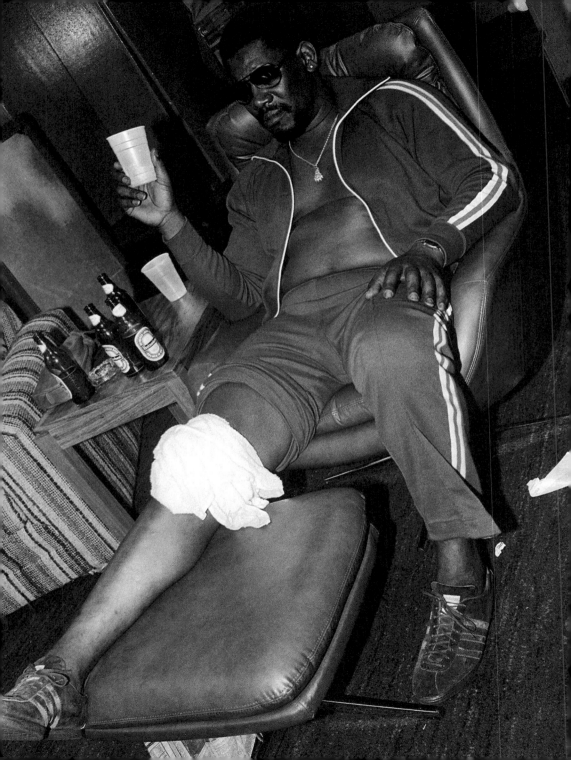

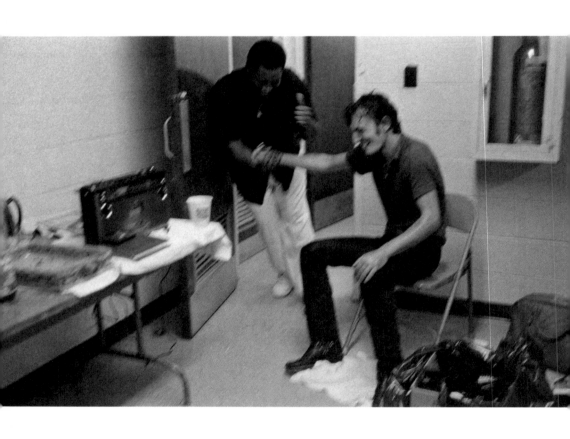

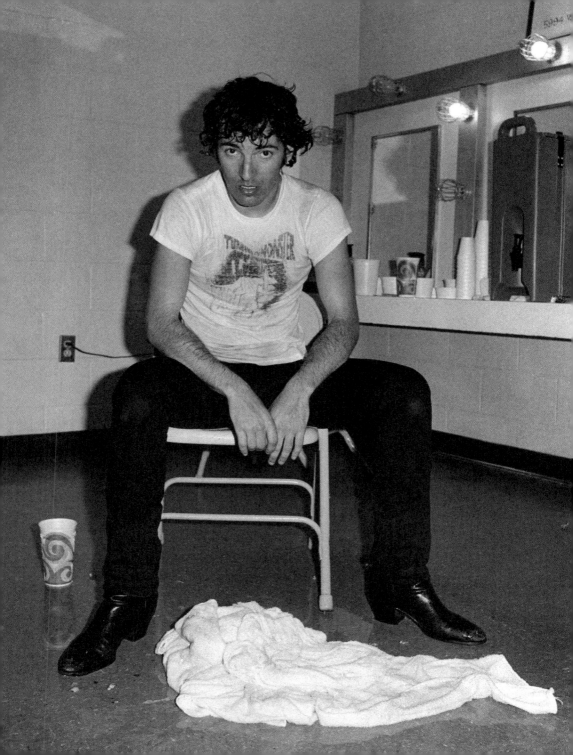

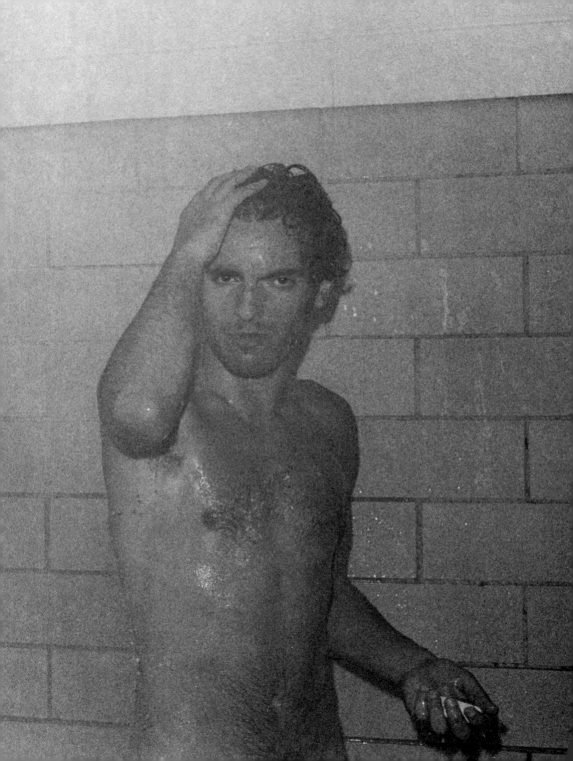

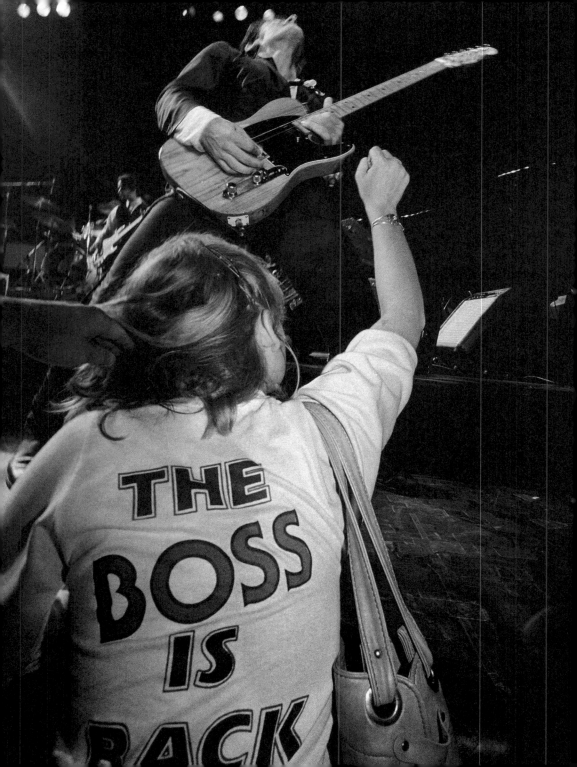

**1978 TOUR
LOCATIONS PICTURED**
Holmdel, New Jersey
New York, New York
Buffalo, New York
Boston, Massachusetts
Philadelphia, Pennsylvania
Uniondale, New York
Bloomington, Minnesota
Iowa City, Iowa
Portland, Oregon
Seattle, Washington
Vancouver, Canada
Dallas, Texas
San Antonio, Texas
Houston, Texas
New Orleans, Louisiana
Jackson, Mississippi
Charleston, West Virginia
Louisville, Kentucky
Kalamazoo, Michigan
Cleveland, Ohio
Detroit, Michigan

**SPECIAL THANKS TO
THE E STREET BAND**
Max Weinberg
Clarence Clemons
Danny Federici
Garry W. Tallent
Roy Bittan
Steve Van Zandt

OTHERS PICTURED
Maureen Van Zandt
Jimmy Iovine
Jon Landau
Adele, Ginny, and
Pam Springsteen

ACKNOWLEDGMENTS
Sid Schneider
Glen O'Brien
Craig Nelson
Robert Haavie

ART DIRECTION / DESIGN
Greg Foley

First published in
the United States of America in 2000
by UNIVERSE PUBLISHING
A Division of
Rizzoli International Publications, Inc.
300 Park Avenue South
New York, NY 10010
photographs©1978, text ©2000 Lynn Goldsmith
All concert photographs, with the exception of page
29, ©1978 Corbis

00 01 02 / 10 9 8 7 6 5 4 3 2 1

Printed in Singapore